D1569755

WE WERE HERE FIRST
THE NATIVE AMERICANS

THE
INUIT
OF THE ARCTIC

TAMRA ORR

PURPLE TOAD
PUBLISHING

P.O. Box 631
Kennett Square, Pennsylvania 19348
www.purpletoadpublishing.com

WE WERE HERE FIRST
THE NATIVE AMERICANS

The Apache of the Southwest
The Inuit of the Arctic
The Iroquois of the Northeast
The Nez Perce of the Pacific Northwest
The Sioux of the Great Northern Plains

Copyright © 2014 by Purple Toad Publishing, Inc.

Printing   1   2   3   4   5   6   7   8   9

Publisher's Cataloging-in-Publication Data
Orr, Tamra
   The Inuit of the Artic / Tamra Orr
      p. cm.—(We were here first. The Native Americans)
Includes bibliographic references and index.
ISBN: 978-1-62469-073-0 (library bound)
1. Inuit—Juvenile literature.   I. Title.
  E99.E7 2013
  979.80049712—dc23
                                                    2013913646
eBook ISBN: 9781624690747

Printed by Lake Book Manufacturing, Chicago, IL

CONTENTS

Holes in the ice are often opportunities for hungry Inuit to wait patiently for the day's dinner to appear.

CHAPTER 1
STAYING PATIENT AND STILL

Anik sat very still next to the *aglu*. He had been waiting all morning and now the sun was high overhead, shining down on him, helping him stay warm in the snow. Anik knew that even though his legs were tired and his eyes were becoming heavier by the passing moment, he must stay awake and aware. Any moment now, a seal would use this breathing hole in the ice to surface and get some air before sinking back down under the frigid waters.

Anik had lost count of how many times he had seen a seal pop up from a hole amid the snow and ice. Every time it had happened, he had either been too far away to reach the aglu in time or did not have his spear or harpoon at hand. This time, however, he was completely prepared. He and several other hunters from his group had headed out before dawn this morning. Anik's dog, Shika, had sniffed out this hole for him. She had let out a single bark to tell him, "A good spot is right here!" Now, she sat quietly and patiently on the snow with him. She knew, somehow, making any sound or movement would spoil the success of the hunt.

Standing still with harpoon in hand takes tremendous patience and control for any age.

With harpoon in hand, Anik settled in to wait. If he had to sit here for days to catch a seal, he would. He imagined the excitement in his band when he returned with food to share with everyone. His people would sing and dance, and celebrate his patience and skill. The joy it would bring—as well as the pride, would be worth the time and the cramped muscles from standing in place, hour after hour. He just hoped he would be the first to capture a seal. It would be his first!

Anik's feet rested on the piece of caribou hide he had brought with him. Keeping his feet on this mat prevented him from making any sounds on the snow as he shifted positions. Those sounds could warn a seal or walrus of danger, so they were not allowed. Absolute silence was the only way to win the hunt. Quietly, Anik checked his pouch to make sure he had his knife and rope close by. He put his hand on the charms sewn onto his parka. He hoped they would bring him good luck today.

Just as the sun was dipping low in the sky and darkness was creeping in at the edges, Anik heard the sound for which he had been waiting for so long. The water rippled and seconds later, a seal's head popped up in the small hole. Anik was ready with his harpoon! He struck and pulled. The seal struggled, but Anik was strong and determined. They battled each other, pulling and pushing on the slippery ice. At last, Anik won.

Seal hunting was one of the Inuit's most important skills. Finding enough food to eat was a constant battle between people and animals.

The other hunters ran over, yelling with happiness at Anik's success. With pride, Anik pulled out his sharp knife and made the first cut. It was tradition for the hunters to have the first taste of the kill, and then take a moment of silence in respect for the seal for giving up its life so the people could survive another day.

Finally, Anik was given the honor of pulling the seal to camp. It was the best trip of his young life. When he arrived in the camp, his wife was waiting for him. Quickly, she melted ice in her mouth and gave it to the seal to show the camp's appreciation of the animal. Finally, Anik placed the harpoon he used next to the lamp inside the family's *igloo*. This ensured that the soul of the animal, which still clung to the harpoon, would remain warm throughout the night hours.

As his wife cut the seal to share with everyone throughout the camp, Anik could not stop smiling. He knew that, thanks to his patience and skill, tonight his people would eat well. They would have fat to use as fuel for their lamps. His wife would have the skin to make a strong pair of boots. He took a moment to thank Sedna, the lady of the sea, for providing for his people. Then, putting on his parka again, he went to join in the feasting and rejoicing.

Inuit women often chewed seal skin to ensure it was soft enough to make a comfortable pair of boots.

The Goddess of the Sea

The lives of the Inuit depended a great deal on the bounty of the oceans. Without sea creatures, it would have been impossible for the people to survive in their harsh environment. Many Inuit gave thanks to Sedna, the lady of the sea, for sharing. Like the mermaids in fairy tales, Sedna had the head and torso of a woman, but the tail of a fish.

The Inuit Sea Goddess

During the winter, every time a seal was caught, the bladder was set aside. As the weather warmed in spring, the bladders were inflated with air, like balloons, and cast off into the sea as a way of showing honor to Sedna's generosity.

Naturally, stories were told in Inuit camps of this wonderful sea goddess. Here is one version.

Once upon a time, Sedna lived in the Arctic with her parents. She had such a wonderful life at home she decided to never marry, even though many men asked permission. Finally, one day she met a man who promised her he would provide all the furs and food she could ever want. They married, and she went to live on his island. There, she discovered her husband was a bird in disguise and all he provided was fish!

When her father came to visit, he saw Sedna's unhappiness, and tried to bring her back home. However, on the way, they were struck by a terrible storm. Fearing he would drown, Sedna's father threw her into the water. When she tried to cling to the boat, he chopped off her fingers. Each one turned into fish, seals, walruses, and whales.

Sedna sank to the ocean floor, where she became a powerful spirit, in charge of all sea creatures. She shares her creatures with the humans above, but to show respect, fresh water must be given to all captured seals before they are eaten.[1]

The Inuit world is made up of vast areas of blinding white, thick snow, only marked by the footprints of the creatures who live nearby.

CHAPTER 2
COAST AND
TUNDRA

Standing next to a hole in the ice for hours and hours took strength, patience, and endurance. All of those were skills the Inuit knew from birth. They had no choice. The places they lived demanded that they be tough, brave, and resilient or they simply would not survive.

Imagine living in areas surrounded by snow and ice almost all year round. It is bitingly cold, with temperatures often averaging 20 to 30 degrees Fahrenheit below zero! The wind never seems to stop blowing across the flat, barren tundra. Windstorms were common, creating huge snow drifts. Very few trees or plants grow because the ground is permanently frozen, except for a brief time in the summer months. Any plants that do manage to grow, like the Arctic willow, are extremely short and remain close to the ground. Otherwise, they would be blown down.

In some places, the sun does not even come up for a good part of the year, and the people live in darkness for months at a time. This earned some of the area the nickname of "Land of the Midnight Sun." In others, closer to the North Pole, the opposite was true. There were months of sunshine, and the sun never fully set.

Igloos were the perfect homes for the early Inuit. The materials to build them never ran out. They could be built quickly and abandoned to nature when no longer needed.

Homes were built along the coastline to be near the ocean and the food it provided. When Inuits could no longer find enough game on land or in the sea, they packed up everything they owned and moved to a new place.

This Native American group lived in regions scattered across over 12,000 square miles of the Arctic Circle. They ranged from Alaska and the islands of the Bering Sea in the West, across Canada and to the coast of Greenland in the East, and even all the way to Russian Siberia. Historians are not sure if the original people first came to these lands on foot, across the land bridge connecting Siberia to Alaska, or by boat, after the bridge was covered by water. They do know that these were some of the last people to make the trip, arriving between 3000 and 2500 BCE.[1]

The first people to live in the Arctic regions were the pre-Dorset group. They arrived around 4,000 years ago from Alaska, and migrated as far as Greenland. This culture was nomadic, moving all the time in search of caribou, fish, and wolves. They were followed by the Dorset group around 800 BCE. The Inuit referred to these people as Tuniit and credit them with making some of the culture's earliest ivory and bone carvings. The third group to travel into the area was the Thule. They arrived between 900 and 1300 CE and remained until the Inuit came into the region around 1750.[2] They split into three main groups. The Alaska group included those in parts of Alaska and Siberia. The Central Inuit encompassed those living in northern Canada, Labrador, and Baffin Island, and the third group settled in Greenland.

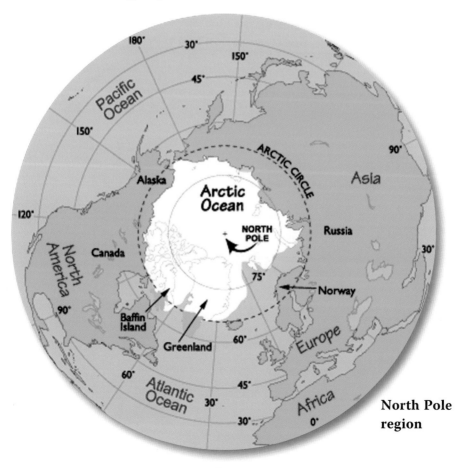

North Pole region

The Inuit were once known as Eskimos. For years, that word was translated by some as "eaters of raw meat," and the Inuit people found the name somewhat offensive. Although later translations indicated that the word may actually have meant "snowshoes," the Inuit still preferred Inuit, which means "the people."

For many years, the Inuit lived in areas so remote that no one else visited. That changed in the late 16th and early 17th centuries when European explorers arrived. They were searching for a route through North America to the Pacific Ocean. Eventually, whaling ships also traveled into Inuit territory. Just as with other Native American tribes, these visits brought change—some good, and some bad.

Whaling ships came searching for the ocean's creatures, but also discovered the Inuit and their culture.

Fur trading helped develop the Inuit's economy, but it carried costs that would change their lives in ways they never expected.

The Inuit happily traded their furs and skins with the Europeans and Americans for rifles and other weapons. The natives were also introduced to tea and flour. During the trades, however, two very dangerous and damaging elements were also exchanged—smallpox and alcohol. By the late 1800s, the Inuit population had fallen to one-third of what it had been due to a combination of illness and alcoholism. Things got even worse because, as the Inuit used faster, more efficient weapons, they killed more and more animals. The population of land and sea creatures began to drop dramatically. This left the Inuit with less to trade with, and they had grown dependent on foreign goods. They moved closer to trading posts, abandoning the traditional nomadic life of moving from one place to another.

All of these changes introduced stresses and made it harder and harder for the Inuit to follow their culture's customs. Children were sent

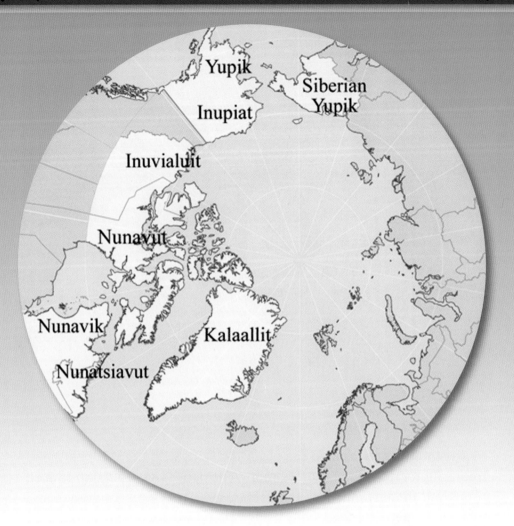

As trading grew, the traveling lifestyle of the Inuit came to an end and soon tribes settled down into specific areas of the Arctic Circle.

to public schools that did not permit them to speak their native language. They spent hours away from their families, exposed to more modern methods and ideas, further creating a divide between the younger and elder generations. Soon, long-held traditions were dropped, and eventually lost. The question was—would these traditions ever be found again?[3]

Lucky Charms

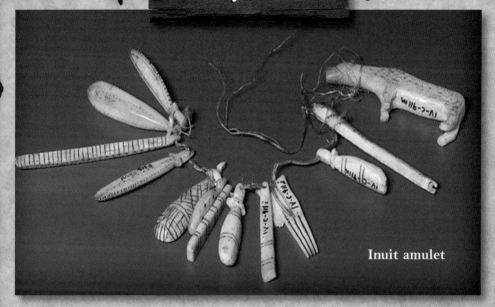

Inuit amulet

Worried about vengeful spirits? Scared that you won't find enough game for your family to eat? Eager to find a life partner? Hoping to honor the soul of a deceased relative? If you were an Inuit, you would take care of all these concerns by wearing amulets, or charms designed to protect you or bring you good luck. You might sew them onto your tent or your dress, belt, or *parka*. Some might be applied to your boat, or attached to the handle of your favorite knife or harpoon. Others were worn as necklaces, or bracelets.

Amulets could be made out of many different materials. Some of the most common included animal teeth, claws, skin, tails, or feet, as well as stones, wooden figures, or ivory carvings. Most amulets were made by the group's shaman. The carvings made in ivory, bone, and wood were done only by men until recent years. Walrus tusks were a favorite material, and carving was done with a sharpened stone. Some drew animals and people, while other artists chose abstract designs. The Inuit believed that wearing these amulets or putting them on their homes, boats, or tools would help guide them to prey, and protect them from danger.[4] Following their superstition that land and sea creatures should never mix, amulets from each type of creature were never worn together.

The Inuit depended heavily on their dogs for moving and hunting.

CHAPTER 3
A BAND ON
THE MOVE

Life on the snow and ice was never easy, and it meant a life on the move. Groups of Inuit, usually all related one way or another, would form a group or band and move together from place to place in search of food. These groups varied in size from a few dozen to a few hundred. The men in these groups spent almost every single day searching for enough food to keep their people alive. They never hunted for land animals and sea creatures on the same trip, as they believed that would anger the spirits. When hunting on land, the men would climb on wooden dogsleds, known as *qamutiks*. These were pulled by their faithful, hardworking team of huskies or *qimiq*. These sleds were often coated with moss or ice to help them slide easily across the snow. Some sleds were short, measuring only a few feet long and pulled by several dogs. Others were much longer, and pulled through the snow by a dozen hardy dogs.

Depending on the area they lived in, some men and their dog teams hunted for geese, ducks, caribou (reindeer), and even polar bears! Others searched for musk oxen, mountain sheep, wolves, fox, hares, or even squirrels. They captured animals by using bows and arrows, spears, and harpoons.

Some Inuit tribes hunted on land as a group. Women and children chased animals with rocks and yelled to make the creatures move. They drove them into the water or to a corral which was a fenced-in area the men had already set up. Once the animals were trapped, the men would kill them quickly and as painlessly as possible.

Off to Sea

On other days, the men would approach the sea in search of food. Like Anik, some might spend hours next to a breathing hole, waiting for a seal to pop up for a quick breath of air. In the spring, when seals would crawl out on the surface of the ice to enjoy the warmth of the sun, some hunters would sneak up on them by crawling on the ice on all fours. For many hours, hunters would slide very slowly across the ice, doing the best they could to not be noticed by the seals. If spotted, the men would freeze, and then pop their heads up and down like the seals. Most parts of the year, hunters would climb inside their one-man kayaks and fish

Fishing nearby oceans was usually done alone in a small, one-person boat.

Teams would work together to search the ocean for bigger prey, including walruses and whales.

with rods made of animal bones. They might also use hand woven nets to capture cod, trout, pike, halibut, and herring. In some areas, fishermen caught eels, crabs, and shellfish, while in others, the people created small dams to capture migrating fish like salmon.

Larger groups used a much bigger boat called an *umiak* to hunt for everything from whales, seals, and walruses to sea lions and narwhals. The umiak held five or six men. Four would paddle, while one helmsman steered the boat. The last person was the one in charge of the harpoon.[1] The men rarely spoke; they knew that they must remain quiet so they wouldn't scare away sea creatures. When prey was spotted, the harpooner would ready his weapon. He had to throw accurately enough to hit it and powerfully enough to break the skin. Once the harpoon was attached to the creature, floats on the rope helped the men in the boat keep track of where it was. The floats also helped tire the creature out. Then, the other men reached out with their spears.[2] It was a dangerous game the Inuit played out on the icy waters. A frightened animal could easily attack the boat and capsize or even destroy it. Everyone had to remain alert and aware.

Heading for Home

Once the sea creature was caught, the umiaks would gather on the water to tow the carcass to shore. Now the silence was over and the men filled the icy air with songs and laughter. They knew they would return to a celebration as the meat and blubber, the layer of fat under the skin, was cut up and shared with everyone in the group. Even the contents of the creature's stomach were eaten, providing the group with foods like seaweed and shrimp.

There was no concept of "mine" and "yours" within the group. The food belonged to everyone, creating a strong feeling of community. This type of cooperation and teamwork meant that no one would go to bed hungry.

The Inuit ate almost all of their meat raw. They would cut strips off whenever they got hungry and chew on them for long periods of time. There were no set meal times. Instead, people grabbed a piece of meat whenever they felt hungry. Only the very toughest meat was cooked, the rest was eaten raw.

No part of an animal was wasted in the Inuit world. One of the Inuit's deepest beliefs was every living creature had a soul and should be given respect. The people thanked the animals, and even gave them gifts. Seals, for example, were given a mouthful of fresh water made from melted ice.[3] The Inuit believed that if an animal was not honored and respected, it could turn into a hostile, angry monster spirit that might attack them on the next hunt. These beliefs carried over into their hunting styles. The hunters never caused unneeded pain to their prey, and often bowed in appreciation after a successful kill.

Sea creatures like walruses and seals were shared with the others. Meat was taken for food, blubber was used for fuel for oil lamps, and skin was used for making clothes. The sinew from land animals was used for thread and lashing together the wood on sleds. Fur was used to create clothing like parkas and boots.[4]

Since the Inuit did not know when they might find their next meal, they often did everything they could to preserve any extra food. Strips of meat were cut and left out to dry in the sun for jerky. Others were stored under rocks to freeze until they were needed. The meat from land animals and the meat from sea creatures were never stored in the same place.

A Breath of Spring

Even though the areas the Inuit lived in were some of the coldest in the world, summer did stop by, although only briefly. During the warmest months of the year, the permafrost would melt just enough to jumpstart the seeds and plants in the soil. Suddenly, the tundra would be filled with the colors of wildflowers. None of the plants grew very tall, or the wind would destroy them. For example, the Arctic willow is a tree that is only a few inches tall in this area. If it were stretched out, it would be over 60 feet tall![5] Within a matter of weeks, plants were a foot tall, growing quickly before the season was over.

A field of Arctic willows appears as a dense, thick, but very short forest.

Caribou moss was so versatile that it could be used for everything from emergency food to insulation against the cold.

Before the warmth of summer passed, the Inuit spent hours gathering the berries that grew. This fruit was a real treat since it was so rare. It was added to dishes to give them a sweeter taste. The people also gathered grasses, lichen, and caribou moss. These were used for fuel or wicks, to feed animals, make mats, and to add a layer of warmth to boots or diapers. During times with very little food, the Inuit even ate these greens to stay alive.

The Inuit were incredibly adaptable, able to make the most of whatever they were able to hunt and pick. Their lifestyle was simple, and almost everything centered on the concepts of survival—and family.

Songs, Stories, and Arguments

The Inuit were a happy people, rejoicing in life and celebrating their heritage by singing songs and telling stories. They even found a way to make arguments into entertainment. Singing was common in the bands of Inuit people. They sang to show happiness at a feast or when the men returned home with game. They

Throat singing

sang to honor the souls of the animals who were killed so that the Inuit could live. They sang as they worked in order to pass the time. They sang to cheer each other up, to accompany a dance, to entertain children, and to tell important stories. Sometimes they even sang to compete with each other and as part of their games. Whoever sang a song for the first time "owned" the song and no one could sing it again without that person's permission.[6]

One particular type of Inuit singing is very unusual. It is typically a competition between two women and is known as "throat singing." The women face each other and begin singing, and the first one who laughs loses. Sometimes the sound is like humming; other times it is like loud breathing with notes in between. It has a strong rhythm, and tends to speed up as the song progresses.[7] Songs were often accompanied by drums made out of caribou skin, or an animal's bladder stretched over a wooden hoop.[8]

Because Inuit groups tended to be small and most were related through either family or marriage, arguments could be difficult. Some were settled by fist fights or wrestling matches. Other groups coped with conflict in another way. Each man involved in the conflict would have his wife sing a song about their version of the disagreement. Instead of just reciting the facts, however, each one had to sing and make the facts as entertaining and funny as possible. The person who achieved the most laughs won the argument![9]

Although igloos look like they would be too
hard and cold to live in, they were actually
comfortable homes for the Inuit.

CHAPTER 4
COOPERATION AND SURVIVAL

Illiquusiq is an Inuit word that means "the ways and habits of the people."[1] The word encompasses the way the Inuit lived, played, dressed, and ate. Without the cooperation of everyone in the group, there would have been no way to survive.

Home, Snowy Homes

Because the Inuit were *nomadic,* and moved frequently, they had to have houses that were quick to put up and take down, and very few possessions. Typically, they lived in two different types of homes, depending on the time of year, and how long they would be staying in an area. One of the most popular temporary homes used in cold weather was the *igloo,* or snow house. It was used by hunters to take shelter in during some of the coldest parts of the winter. Most only took less than a half hour to build from start to finish.[2]

An igloo is made of blocks of snow that are placed in a circle. Each layer that is added is slightly smaller than the last until they meet at the top, creating a dome shape. Any cracks or holes are filled with more snow. A hole is left open to use as a smoke vent. Igloos had long, low entrances to help keep the cold winds out. Inside, these igloos often had benches and

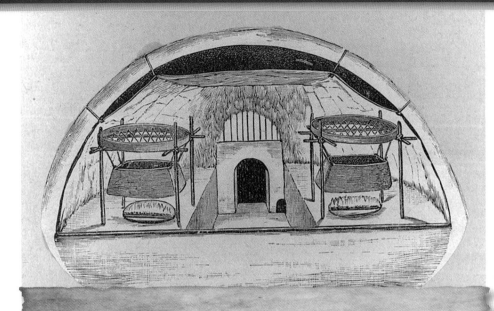

Inside, igloos were designed to make the most of the limited space they had available. One room functioned as a kitchen, living room, and bedroom for the family.

tables made out of snow. They were covered with branches and fur for sitting and sleeping on comfortably.

Oil lamps that burned with melted seal and whale oil provided light inside. The smoke went out the vent, while the heat from the lamp melted the inside just enough to create a layer of ice. This provided even more insulation from the harsh weather outside.

During the warmer part of the year, the Inuit built tent homes from animal skins and driftwood poles. These homes were very similar to the teepees used by other Native American tribes. Wood was hard to find in these cold and desolate regions, so the poles were treasured. Some people used whale bones for their frame. Caribou or seal skin was stretched over the poles, and kept in place by a ring of rocks around the bottom.

The Inuit who lived in the western regions of Canada had more access to trees, so some built log homes. These houses were built over a pit dug into the ground. Poles were put up, and logs and sod were piled all the way to the top. With part of the house underground, the people were protected from the wind.

Families had very few possessions. There was little to have and no room to keep it if they did. Almost everything in the Inuit group was communal, or shared. The only exceptions were the men's tools and the clothing the women made for their families.

Staying Warm

Finding enough food to eat was the primary job for the Inuit men. At the same time, the Inuit women worked hard to ensure the hunters had the right clothes to keep them warm. This took a great deal of time and skill.

Most of the Inuit wore the same type of clothes. Men, women, and children wore large parkas that had built-in hoods. Women had slightly larger parkas called *amautis* so that they could carry babies on their backs underneath. Men and women wore pants, and everyone wore mittens, and waterproof boots.[3]

Each piece of clothing was made from animal skins and fur. The inner layer used a finer, softer fur, while the outside layer was much thicker.

Inuit family

The clothing was coated in fish oil to help make it waterproof. Often, it was also decorated with bird feathers, beads, embroidery, and amulets. Seams were sewn together with sinew thread, using an ivory or bone needle. Everything had to be extremely tight, because no hunter could survive getting wet in below-zero temperatures. Some Inuit used the intestines of mammals instead of skins because they tended to be extra waterproof.

Mittens were essential for keeping hands warm, and like the rest of the clothing, were made of a combination of skins and fur. Boots were called *mukluks*. Feet were at high risk of getting frostbite, so a number of steps were taken to protect them. First, the Inuit put on a stocking, then a mukluk, and then, finally, a fur slipper. Frequently they were lined with layers of moss for extra warmth. All three of these commonly reached up the leg to the knee, and even to the thigh.[4]

Every piece of clothing was custom fit so it would not be too large. Clothing that was too big carried the risk of water, snow, ice, and wind getting in. Many Inuit wore a belt around their waists. It held pouches for knives and other tools.

The final part of the Inuit wardrobe was snow goggles, known as *ggaak*. Originally, they were made with round pieces of wood with tiny slits cut into them. Others were made of caribou antlers. They protected the face, but more importantly, they protected the Inuit's eyes and prevented snow blindness—a temporary blindness due to exposure to bright sunlight reflected off of snow and ice.[5]

From Birth to Death

Inuit groups ranged in size, but they all tended to be related to each other in some way, by blood or marriage. Parents and children lived together, sometimes with both sets of grandparents. If the group had more of one gender than another, some families might be made up of multiple husbands or multiple wives.

Family was extremely important to the Inuit, and children were cherished. A special birthing tent was often created for women. If a woman went into labor while the group was on the move, she would drop back, have the baby as quickly as possible, and then catch up. Often she and the baby would be allowed to ride in one of the sleds.[6]

Babies were carried on the mother's back for more than a year, and nursed for several years. All children slept near their mothers in order to stay warm. Babies were cuddled often. Punishment was almost never used. Inuit children knew what was expected of them, and they were given a great deal of freedom to run, play, and have fun. The Inuit believed that each baby was born with the soul of a relative and so, early in life, children were given the same respect and treatment as adults. Adults watched over the children, making sure they were safe.[7]

Girls were ready for marriage as soon as they reached puberty. This was often signaled by placing a tattoo on a girl's chin.[8] Boys were ready once they had proven they could hunt and provide for a family. This was often indicated with a tattoo as well. Boys were given tattoos of small dots on a joint, such as an elbow, wrist, ankle, or hip once they had made their first kill.

Tattoos were used by the Inuit to indicate when young people were ready for marriage.

There was no marriage ceremony for a couple. Instead, they simply moved in together. Often these relationships had been decided by the children's parents years earlier. Couples did not hug or kiss in public. That type of behavior was reserved for small children. If a couple's marriage did not work out, they separated and were considered divorced. The Inuit do not have any set rules or government, so individuals make their own decisions.

In a family, men were expected to hunt for food, make tools and weapons, build shelters, take care of sled dogs, and protect the family. The women's role, on the other hand, centered around raising children, preparing food, cleaning, and making clothing, boots, and tents.

It is little surprise that the Inuit did not live extremely long lives. The environment was too harsh to live much longer than 40 or 50 years. Old age was respected, and the Inuit often sought the advice of their elders.

Thanks to years of chewing on skins for use in boots and clothing, adult Inuit women often had flat teeth.

Sometimes old age was perceived as a burden because the elderly reached a point where they could not do their jobs, or keep up when the group had to move. When older people died, they could not be buried because the ground was simply too hard and frozen. Instead, they were laid out for several days and then covered with stones and driftwood. [9]

During the mourning period, the women did not do any sewing. They also did not comb their hair. Once a person died, no one could speak his or

Inuit medicine man and boy, 1900

her name aloud, or else his or her spirit might come back as an evil one determined to cause harm to others. Many of the Inuit believed that when people died, their souls went into the next child born.

Much of the Inuit beliefs came from the group's shaman or *angekkok,* a man or woman who was considered a connection to the spirits and gods. The shaman trained for years and years learning to sing, dance, and play the drums, plus how to communicate with gods. The shaman would go into a trance to visit the spirit world to find a cure or a solution to a problem. He would return from this state to make predictions that were respected—and sometimes feared—by the entire group. [10]

One of the greatest threats to Inuit culture was the arrival of far-reaching poverty. It threatened their way of life in countless ways.

As wise as the shaman was, he was not able to predict what was going to happen to primitive Inuit culture. After the arrival of the Europeans, others followed. In the late 1860s, the Canadian government had control over much of the Inuit territory. The Inuit grew increasingly dependent on foreign trade and on the Canadian and U. S. governments for basic needs, such as food, shelter, and medical care. Poverty became common. Religious beliefs in spirits began to fade as the foreigners constantly broke taboos and rules, yet were not punished. As time passed, it was inevitable that the Inuit culture could not last.

The Inuit Language

Although the different groups of Inuit were scattered across thousands of miles, their language remained similar enough that one group could easily understand another's words. The Inuit often used the same base or root word and then kept adding prefixes and suffixes to further describe something. For example, the Inuit are said to have 100 words to describe snow. Based on the root of "tla" which simply means "snow," here are some of them:

tlapa	powder snow
talcringit	snow that is crusted on the surface
talpat	still snow
tlamo	snow that falls in large, wet flakes
tlatim	snow that falls in small flakes
tlaslo	snow that falls slowly
tlapinti	snow that falls quickly
blotla	blowing snow
slimtla	snow crusted on top and soft underneath
allatla	baked snow
jatla	snow between your fingers or toes
kriyantli	snow bricks
intla	snow that has drifted inside
nootlin	snow that doesn't stick
tlalam	snow sold to American tourists[11]

Inuit writing was largely made up of symbols. This is a sample text in *Inuktitu*, or Inuit language.

> ᐃᓄᖕᒍᑦ ᐃᓅᑦᓯᐅᖅᑐᒥ ᓇᒡᒐᓇᒡᒍᕐᒪᖃᖅᑐᓄᑦ ᐊᓯᖏᓪᓗ
> ᐃᓕᑕᕆᐅᕐᓇᕐᔭᑦᐋᖅᑐᓄᑦᓗ ᐱᕐᓇᖅᐅᑎᑕᖅᑐᖅᑐᓄᑦ.
> ᐃᓯᒪᕐᕋᕐᖅᑭᐅᕋᑕᕐᓇᐋᑐᓂᕐᒥᕐ ᐊᖂᑎᐊᖁᑎᕐᔭᕐᑦ ᐱᑕᕐᑐᕐᐅᐱᐅᕐ, ᐊᑉᐊᕐᑐᔭᕐᐋᓪᓗ
> ᐃᓚᑐᕐᓂᐊᕐᑲᖅᑲᑎᖅᑮᐱᐊᖃᕐᑎᓐᐊᔭᕐᔭᕐᐋᖅᑎ ᕠᕋᔭᑎᖅᑎᖅᐅᑎᑳᑦ ᐊᐅᓂᕐᒪᖁᑕ.
> (ᑎᑎᕐᖃᖅᒍᓚᕐᔨᕐ 1 ᑭᒍᑐᐋᕐᐊᐋᖢᕐ ᐱᕐᓇᕐ ᖅᑎᕆᐢ ᐧᕆ ᔭᕐᕠᕋᐱᖅᖃᑎᐢᒪᕐ
> ᐊᔪᐊᐃᕐᖃᕕᕐᔨᓂᕐ)

This is translated as "All human beings are born free and equal in dignity and rights. They are endowed with reason and conscience and should act towards one another in a spirit of brotherhood."[12]

The modern Inuit community is full of small homes, rather than snowy igloos. However, some traditions are still in place.

CHAPTER 5
MIXING OLD AND NEW

The Inuit's *illiquusiq* began to change as soon as Europeans and Americans discovered their culture. Over time, due to the introduction of technology and modern materials, old ways were lost. Sleds were replaced by snowmobiles. Kayaks and umiaks were replaced by motorboats. Igloos and tents were replaced by wooden houses referred to as "matchboxes." Hunting was replaced by trading and grocery stores. Many traditions handed down through generations looked like they would be lost. However, thanks to the efforts of a number of people and organizations, changes have been put in place to preserve the hallmarks of this unusual culture.

Life for the Inuit changed far more when groups began to battle to take over their land. In the late 1950s, the Atomic Energy Commission wanted to use 1,600 square miles to create a deep-water port, and the Inuit fought against it, and won. Over the next few years, a number of Alaska-based organizations were created to protect native territory.[1]

The land became even more valuable when oil was discovered on the North Slope in Alaska. The right to access this oil and build an Alaskan pipeline was settled in 1971 with the Alaska Native Claims Settlement (ANCSA). This act resulted in the Inuit and other natives trading 335 million acres of land in return for $962.5 million. In 1980, it was amended to indicate that natives had the rights to hunt and fish on the land.[2]

Welcome to Nunavut

Fortunately, despite the passing of time, the introduction of other cultures, and the discovery of plentiful oil supplies, the Inuit have managed to hold on to important elements of their heritage. One of the primary ways they did this was through the establishment of Nunavut in Canada.

The idea for Nunavut, or "our land," was first proposed in 1973 by a group called the Inuit Tapirisat of Canada. It took years of discussion, negotiation, and paperwork, but Nunavut territory was officially established on April 1, 1999.[3] The Inuit were given $1.4 billion in order to develop the territory. In exchange, they gave up their claims on all other Canadian lands.

Nunavut is a unique place located in northeastern Canada. It is bordered by Manitoba in the South, the Northwest Territories in the Northwest and West, the Arctic Ocean in the North, Greenland in the Northeast, and the Atlantic Ocean and Quebec in the East.[4] Covering 808,000 square miles, it is divided into three regions known as Qikiqyaaluk, Kivalliq, and Kitikemeot. It is about the size of Alaska and Texas put together. The land includes 12 of Canada's largest islands, and almost three-quarters of the country's coastline.[5]

As of autumn 2011, over 30,000 people lived in Nunavut and 85 percent identified as Inuit. The majority of the people are young, with only six percent over the age of 60.[6] The territory is divided up into 25 communities, which range in size just like in the Inuit's past. The smallest, Grise Fiord, has 130 people, while the largest has 6,699 people and is found in the capital of the region, Iqaluit.[7] These communities are so spread out that they are not connected by roads. Travel between them requires a snowmobile, a ship, or an airplane.

Nunavut's flag is red, yellow, white, and blue. The red shape in the middle is known as the *inukshuk,* which is a very popular symbol for the

Navanut flag

Inuit. It is used to represent the stone monuments that the Inuit would build to either guide people to safety or to mark a sacred place. The red color symbolizes Canada, while the blue and gold are used to honor the riches of the land, sea, and sky. The blue star on the top right corner is a symbol for the North Star, or *Niqirtsuituq*. It represents guidance and leadership.[8]

Nunavut is not only a place for the Inuit to live, but also a way to preserve so much of their unique and important heritage. In recent years, the public schools have been designed to teach children arts and crafts from the past, including Inuit traditions and language. In 2008, the territory's government passed a new education act that would help classrooms focus on traditional knowledge. Under the provisions of this act, Inuit elders were brought into the school to teach skills like building dog sleds, or constructing an igloo. As the Premier of Nunavut, Eva Aariak, says, "Look at kayaks, at the shape of an igloo—no scientist around the world can improve upon their architecture."[9] Some of Nanuvut's schools also offer a program where students can spend up to three weeks on the land with elders, learning hands-on skills. They are taught how to hunt, fish, travel safely, make clothing, and most importantly, how to treat the land with caution and respect.[10]

Modern Inuits are a blend of yesterday's tradition and today's culture.

Challenges Ahead

Today's Inuit face many changes. The effects of global warming have become a significant problem for some. As ice melts, wildlife change their routes, making hunting more difficult. With less meat, many Inuit have come to depend heavily on store bought food—often the less-than-healthy kinds. "The stores only have food that's easy to transport and doesn't perish, so there are no vegetables," reports Barry Smit, a professor at the University of Guelph, Canada, to CNN. "But because of new difficulties in hunting, young people are increasingly eating highly processed junk food, so we are seeing more teeth problems, and obesity."[11] In addition, it costs a great deal to ship fresh foods to the outlying areas where the Inuit live, and the cost is often too much for most families to afford.

The Inuit are a people in transition. While living in the modern world of the present, they are also working hard to maintain the traditions and skills of the past. Finding a way to balance them is difficult, but for people who could remain motionless on the ice hour after hour, it is a challenge they will most likely meet.

Welcome to the Arctic Winter Games

More than 40 years ago, the first Arctic Winter Games was held in Yellowknife, capital of the Northwest Territories. Unlike other competitions, this one only featured athletes from the northern regions of the world. That year, about 500 athletes participated. Since then, the games have continued to grow.

The athletes in today's Arctic Games come from Greenland, Alaska, Russia, Iceland, Northern Scandinavia, and Northern Canada. People compete in a mix of sports including traditional ones such as basketball, badminton, hockey, indoor soccer, table tennis, volleyball, and wrestling. However, other events include alpine skiing, snowboarding, cross-country skiing, snowshoeing, speed skating, and dog mushing. Winners are given the "Ulu medal," which are knives made in gold, silver, and bronze.

The Inuit games are made up of eleven events and each one of them is extremely challenging. They include the:

- one-foot high kick
- two-foot high kick
- airplane
- knuckle hop
- Alaskan high kick
- one-hand reach
- head pull
- arm pull
- sledge jump
- triple jump

Each one of these skills requires a great deal of strength and concentration. They are very difficult to do and require hours of practice. For example, the arm pull begins with two players facing each other on the floor. Each one must keep their left leg straight, while they bend their right leg over the opponent's straight leg. Players lock their right arms together at the elbow, while also holding their opponent's right ankle with their left hand. At the signal, the players start pulling from inside their opponent's elbow. They brace their opposite hand on the other person's leg, foot, or ankle.

Three rounds are played. One arm is used in round one; the opposite one is used in round two, and then reversed again for round three. How does a person win this game? In at least two rounds, one player has to either pull his opponent over, or get his arm to straighten. Imagine the strength this would take. Can you imagine how this skill might have made the Inuit a stronger fighter when wrestling a slippery seal on the ice?[12]

- There are approximately 150,000 Inuit living today. One-third live in Greenland, one-one third in Canada, and another third in Alaska. (A few live in Russia.)

- One of the Inuit's favorite games was jumping on a trampoline, which was made out of a stretched-out walrus skin.

- An Inuit child's toys were just miniature tools, such as weapons and needles.

- Some igloos were built close enough to each other to have a tunnel in between. This allowed people to visit each other without going outside.

- A single person in the Inuit tribe was called an "inuk."

- In 2006, Cape Dorset in Nanavut was voted the most artistic city in Canada.

- The Inuit often ate seafood and seaweed found in the stomachs of sea creatures they killed. They also enjoyed a dish called blood soup.

- Dogs used to pull Inuit sleds were a breed called huskies. They were typically fed one pound of meat and a quarter pound of fat per day.

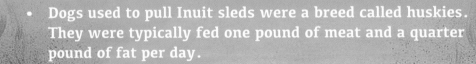

Chapter 1

1. Charles Moore, *Keeveeok, Awake!* Edmonton: Ring House Gallery, 1986, pp. 9–10.

Chapter 2

1. *Nunavut Tourism,* "People of Nunavut." http://www.nunavuttourism.com/people_of_nunavut.aspx

2. "Inuit History," *Scholastic.com,* http://www.scholastic.com/teachers/article/inuit-history

3. *Pauktuutit Inuit Women of Canada,* "The Inuit Way: A Guide to Inuit Culture," 2006. http://www.uqar.ca/files/boreas/inuitway_e.pdf

4. Raymond Bial, *The Inuit,* Tarrytown, NY: Marshall Cavendish, 2002, p. 44.

Chapter 3

1. *Canada's First Peoples.* "The Inuit." http://firstpeoplesofcanada.com/fp_groups/fp_inuit4.html

2. Bial, p. 50.

3. Moore, pp. 9–10.

4. Bial, p. 61.

5. Danielle Corrveau, *The Inuit of Canada.* Minneapolis, MN: Lerner Publications, 2002, p. 10.

6. *Scholastic,* http://www.scholastic.com/teachers/article/inuit-culture-and-legends

7. "Throat Singing," Inuit Cultural Online Resource, http://icor.ottawainuitchildrens.com/node/30

8. Canada's First Peoples, http://firstpeoplesofcanada.com/fp_groups/fp_inuit5.html

9. Corrveau, p. 33.

Chapter 4

1. *Scholastic,* http://www.scholastic.com/teachers/article/inuit-culture-and-legends

2. Canada's First Peoples, http://firstpeoplesofcanada.com/fp_groups/fp_inuit2.html

3. Ibid.

4. Ibid.

5. "Snow Goggles helped Arctic People Survive," *Science Buzz,* http://www.sciencebuzz.org/museum/object/2007_12_snowgoggles

6. *Pauktuutit Inuit Women of Canada.*

7. Ibid.

8. "Arctic & Alaska," The World's Largest Online Tattoo Museum, http://www.vanishingtattoo.com/tattoo_museum/arctic_alaskan_tattoos.html

9. Bial, p. 49.

10. Cottie Burland, "Library of the World's Myths and Legends," *North American Indian Mythology,* (Revised by Marion Wood) New York: Peter Bedrick Books, 1965, pp. 19–20.

11. "Inuit Words for Snow," Mendosa.com, April 15, 2005. http://www.mendosa.com/snow.html

12. "Inuktitut Syllabary," *Omniglot Online Encyclopedia of Writing Systems and Languages,* http://www.omniglot.com/writing/inuktitut.htm

Chapter 5

1. Sydney J. Jones, "Inuit," *Countries and their Cultures,* http://www.everyculture.com/multi/Ha-La/Inuit.html

2. Ibid.

3. "Government of Nunavut," Government of Nunavut Communications, March 2012, http://www.gov.nu.ca/files/Creation%20of%20Nunavut.pdf

4. Corrveau, pp. 22–23.

5. *Nunavut Tourism,* http://www.nunavuttourism.com/people_of_nunavut.aspx

6. Ibid.

7. "Government of Nunavut."

8. Inuit Flag, http://www.indians.org/articles/inuit-flag.html

9. Craig and Marc Kielburger, "Nunavut Education—Old Wisdom in New School," *WE Day,* December 10, 2012, http://www.weday.com/global-voices/nunavut-education-old-wisdom-in-new-school/

10. *Pauktuutit Inuit Women of Canada.*

11. Carriona Davies, "Inuit Lives and Diets Change as Ice Shifts," *CNN,* December 30, 2010, http://www.cnn.com/2010/WORLD/americas/12/30/inuit.impact.climate.change/index.html

12. "Arctic Winter Games," *Aboriginal Affairs and Northern Development Canada,* http://www.aadnc-aandc.gc.ca/eng/1303132383681/1303132625524

Books

Bial, Raymond. *The Inuit.* Tarrytown, NY: Marshall Cavendish, 2002.

Burland, Cottie. "Library of the World's Myths and Legends." *North American Indian Mythology.* (Revised by Marion Wood) New York. Peter Bedrick Books, 1965.

Corrveau, Danielle. *The Inuit of Canada.* Minneapolis, MN: Lerner Publications, 2002.

King, David C. *The Inuit.* Tarrytown, NY: Marshall Cavendish, 2008.

Pauktuutit Inuit Women of Canada, "The Inuit Way: A Guide to Inuit Culture." 2006. http://www.uqar.ca/files/boreas/inuitway_e.pdf

Wolfson, Evely. *Inuit Mythology.* Berkeley Heights, NJ: Enslow Publishers, 2001.

Works Consulted

Davies, Carriona. "Inuit Lives and Diets Change as Ice Shifts." *CNN.* December 30, 2010. http://www.cnn.com/2010/WORLD/americas/12/30/inuit.impact.climate.change/index.html

Effland, Richard. "The Arctic People: Inuit." Mesa Community College. http://web.mesacc.edu/dept/d10/asb/anthro2003/lifeways/inuit/intro.html

"Hunter on Ice." University of Alberta. http://webdocs.cs.ualberta.ca/~vis/models/sealhunt/culture.html

"Inuit Culture, Traditions, and History." Window to the World. National Earth Science Teachers' Association. www.windows2universe.org/earth/polar/inuit_culture.html

"Inuit Culture." University of Waterloo. anthropology.uwaterloo.ca/ArcticArchStuff/Inuit.html

"Inuit History." History for Kids. www.historyforkids.org/learn/northamerica/before1500/history/inuit.htm

"Inuktitut Syllabary." Omniglot Online Encyclopedia of Writing Systems and Languages. http://www.omniglot.com/writing/inuktitut.htm

James, Phil. "The Eskimos' Hundred Words for Snow." State University of New York at Buffalo. Department of Philosophy. http://ontology.buffalo.edu/smith/varia/snow.html

Jones, K. Sydney. "Inuit." Every Culture. www.everyculture.com/multi/Ha-La/Inuit.html#b

Kielburger, Craig and Marc. "Nunavut Education—Old Wisdom in New School." WE Day. December 10, 2012. http://www.weday.com/global-voices/nunavut-education-old-wisdom-in-new-school/

Moore, Charles. *Keeveeok, Awake!* Edmonton: Ring House Gallery, 1986. http://www.polarlife.ca/traditional/myth/sedna.htm

On the Internet

All About the Inuit: For Kids!

> https://sites.google.com/site/inuitforkids/

EcoKids: First Nations & Inuit

> http://www.ecokids.ca/pub/homework_help/first_nations/

The Inuit

> www.encyclopedia.com/topic/Inuit.aspx

Native Americans: Inuit Peoples

> http://www.ducksters.com/history/native_americans/inuit_peoples.php

Two brothers and their kayak

aglu—Breathing hole in the ice used by seals and other oxygen-breathing animals in the ocean.

amautis—A large parka worn by Inuit women to carry their babies on their backs.

amulet—Bracelet or necklace that works as a lucky charm.

angekkok—Inuit for "shaman."

blubber—Layer of fat between skin and muscles.

communal—Describing something done together as a group.

ggaak—Inuit for "snow goggles."

igloo—A home that is made of snow and ice.

illiquusiq—Inuit for "ways and habits."

insulation—A layer added for warmth.

inukshuk—Sacred Inuit object used for guidance.

Inuktitu—The Inuit language.

jerky—Strips of dried meat.

kayak—Single passenger boat.

mukluks—Inuit boots.

niqirtsuituq—Inuit for "North Star."

nomadic—Constantly on the move.

parka—Large coat worn by Inuit men.

permafrost—Permanently frozen layer of soil.

qamutiks—Dog sleds.

qimiq—Sled dogs.

resilient—Flexible and durable.

shaman—Holy man in touch with gods and spirits.

sinew—Animal connective tissue used for thread.

snow blindness—Inability to see due to light reflected off snow and ice.

taboo—Prohibited by social custom.

tundra—Flat, barren ground.

umiak—Large Inuit boat.

ABOUT THE
AUTHOR

Tamra Orr is a full-time writer and author living in the Pacific Northwest. She has written over 300 nonfiction books for readers of all ages. She has a degree in English and Education, and graduated from Ball State University. Orr is the mother of four children, an avid reader, and letter writer. She loves learning about the history of different cultures, and looks forward to learning something new every day of her life.